VENOMOUS ANIMALS OF THE WORLD: THIRD GRADE SCIENCE SERIES

SPEEDY
PUBLISHING

Speedy Publishing LLC
40 E. Main St. #1156
Newark, DE 19711
www.speedypublishing.com

A venom is a a poisonous substance secreted by animals such as snakes, spiders, and scorpions and typically injected into prey or aggressors by biting or stinging.

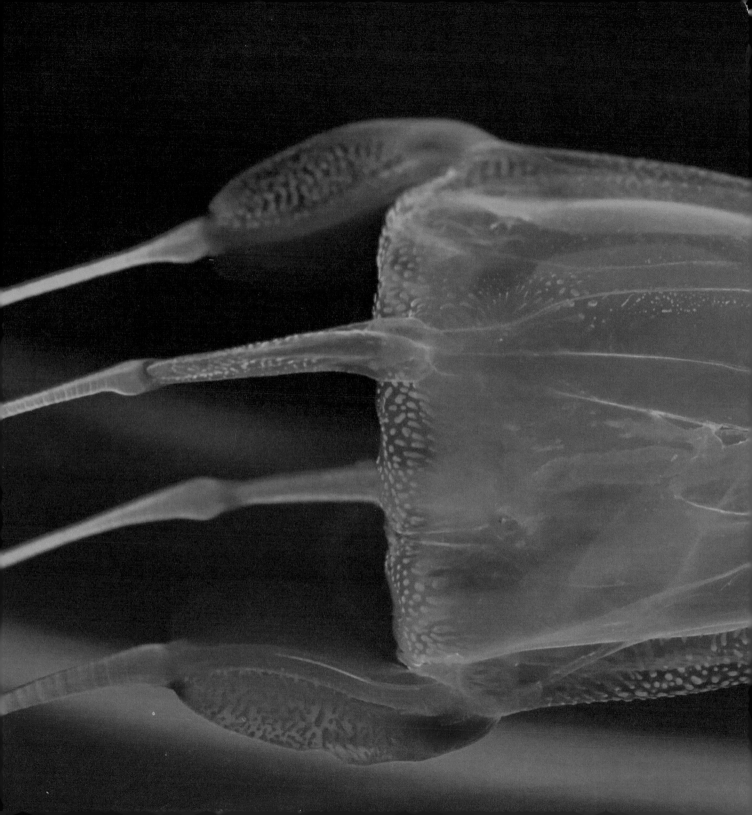

Box jellyfish is one of the most dangerous of all species of Jellyfish in the world. Box jellyfish can move more rapidly than other jellyfish.

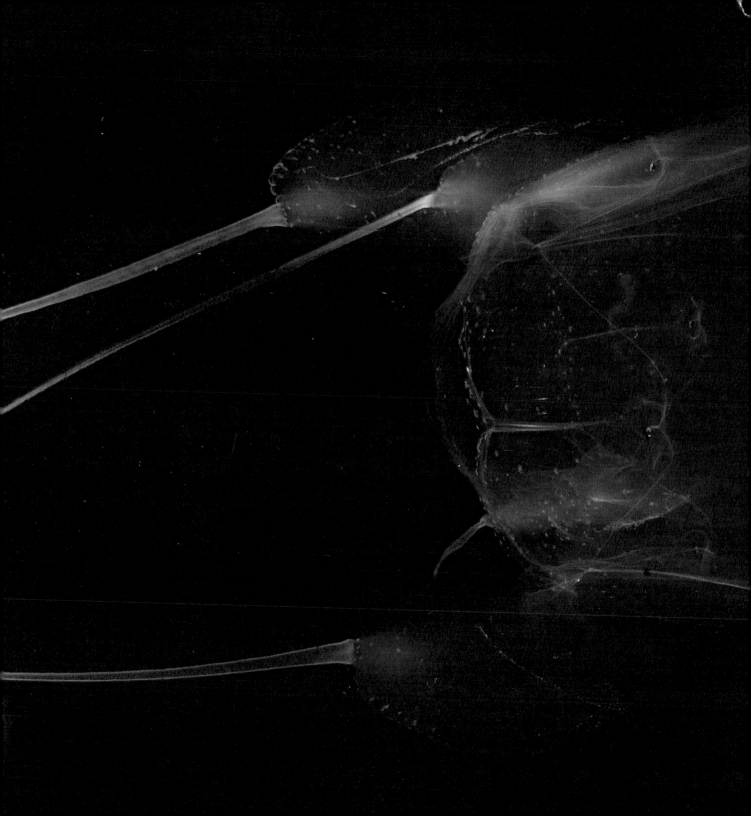

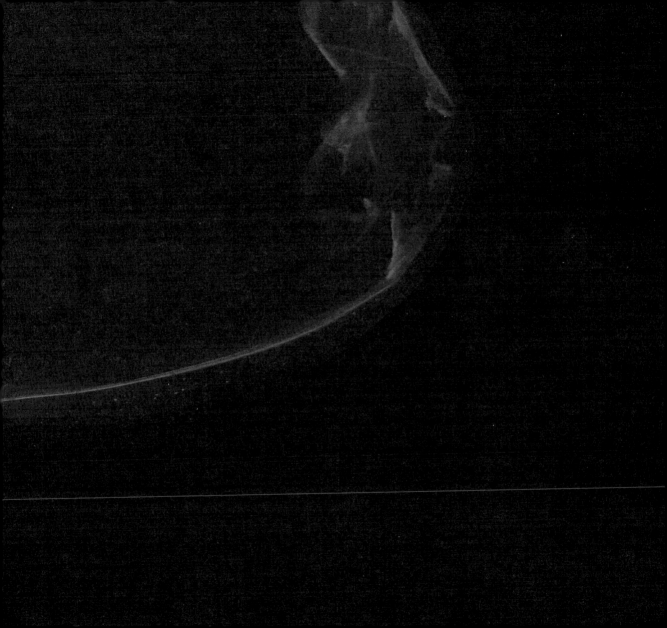

Cobra can raise the front portion of their bodies, while they continue to move. Cobras can't hear sounds in the air, but they feel vibrations on the ground.

The blue-ringed octopus is only the size of a golf ball. Its venom is powerful enough to kill 26 adult humans within minutes.

The deathstalker
is regarded
as the most
dangerous species
of scorpion.
Its venom is a
powerful mixture
of neurotoxins
which causes
an intense and
unbearable pain.

The black mamba is a venomous snake endemic to sub-Saharan Africa. The venom of the black mamba is highly toxic, potentially causing collapse in humans within 45 minutes or less.

Brazilian wandering spider are mainly found in tropical South America. The Brazilian wandering spider is considered as the world's most venomous spider.

Stonefish is the
most venomous
fish in the world.
Venom is produced
in the gland located
in the base of
each spine.

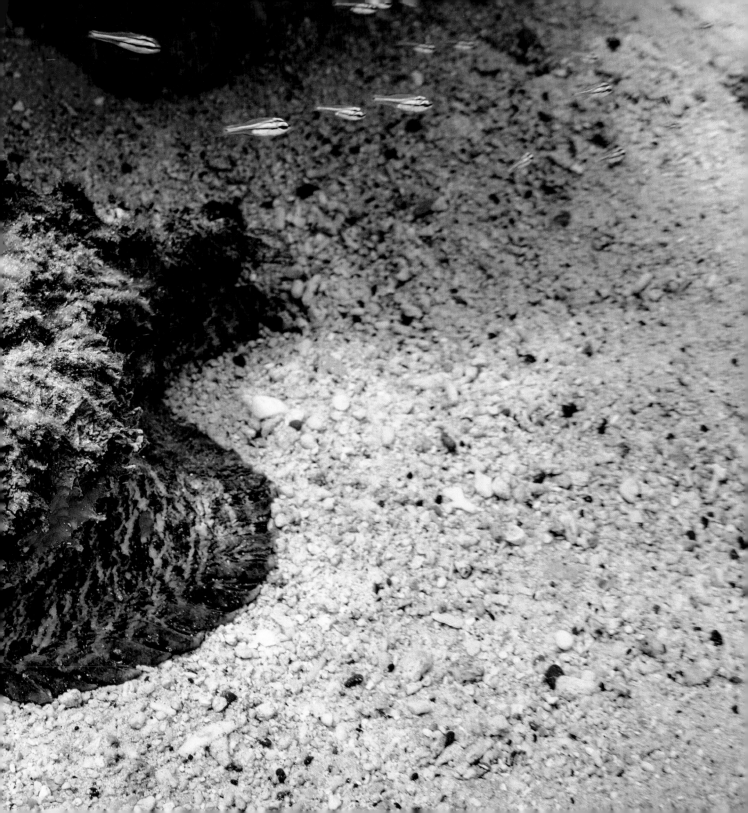

Made in United States
North Haven, CT
29 April 2023

36055766R00020